Philoearth Two

Brendan Banister

Copyright © 2021 Brendan Banister

All rights reserved.

ISBN: 9798733580616

DEDICATION

Dedicated to Future Generations

ACKNOWLEDGMENTS

Thanks to all my teachers, friends and family, and all the people who have helped me without my knowing.

PHILOEARTH TWO

Sometimes I can see Beauty in the world, but sometimes I can't. In this case I'm not talking about my perspective of the world, but rather actually being able to see beauty. I remember when I was a kid, the natural world seemed marvelous, as did many cultural buildings, paintings, and other beautiful Creations by people. Then as a late teenager, I hit some heavy stuff in my life, and sometimes I felt numb. It was as if the natural world became blurry. All Beauty was blurry. I knew it existed, but I could not seem to connect to it. There were also times when I couldn't cry or express my emotions. Growing up I went on many backpacking trips, and at first it took no time at all to connect with the natural world and see the beauty in it. After a while it took longer and longer to connect with the natural world when I would go backpacking. I remember at one point, it took me three days to unwind, slow down, and really begin to soak in where I was. Beauty seems to be a good word, but partially insufficient. Amazing Glory might be a better term for what I experienced when I went backpacking. Letting this Glory soak into my bones was a blissful experience that I didn't want to ever forget. As an adult, I caught glimpses from time to time of the beauty in the world. Mostly, I couldn't slow down enough to really soak it in. Even today, it seems as if there's a film; a translucent barrier between me and the tree outside my window. The window is not much of a barrier, but this cloud around me is a barrier. I can't see very deeply into the life force that is ebbing and flowing and swirling through the tree. While some people might experience a more visual sense of this life force, for me it is a sense of feeling that I'm talking about. I want to dive into the tree and let its beautiful spirit of growth enter into me. I must have been 22 or 23 when I said to myself, "I can't not see the clouds anymore." It may seem like a strange sentence, but I don't think I will ever forget that day. I was so angry that I couldn't see the beauty in the world anymore. I could not tolerate it. I needed to be able to connect with the clouds and all of the beauty in the world, including natural and human Beauty. "I can't not see the clouds anymore." I knew I needed help, so I stayed at 10 different monasteries. That helped a lot. I also kept hiking and doing backpacking trips. I even led backpacking trips for teenagers in three different summer camps. All of this helped some, but not enough. I am simply imploring myself and the world to find a way to connect with each other again. I think that too often, a person is tempted to only write when they feel they have discovered something that is worthwhile; when they have graduated from some Challenge or dilemma. I don't have any magic key. Maybe no one does. Not all stories have a happy ending, but some do. I think stories with a happy ending are becoming more and more rare these days. I do want to improve my connection with the world, and I do want to share the insights that I gain along the way. The same goes for learning from others. When things are working for other people, I want them to share with me. That being said, I think it is too destination oriented to wait on expressing something until there is some final attainment or enlightenment. While I don't have a magic key for connecting with the world, I do think that connecting with the world is a key to improve our quality of life and to benefit all beings. It is so important. We have this idea that long ago people were more connected with the world. They were more in tune with nature, more appreciative of beauty, and took time for what was really important. I think to a large degree this is true, but I also think that living in distraction was not invented yesterday. There is an old

Native American story that I want to bring up. There are many stories about coyote. In this story, coyote wants to marry his daughter. The way I remember it is that coyote goes away from the house and dresses up in a disguise. Then he comes to the house in the disguise and wants to marry the daughter. Then he goes away again and takes off the disguise. He comes back and encourages his daughter to marry that other coyote. Then he goes back out again and comes back with the disguise and marries the daughter. There are several ways to look at this story. One could idealize coyote and how clever he was, which is not a good idea. One could be disgusted and learn from the story what needs to be avoided. There are many fairy tales and old folk tales that show the evil that humans are capable of. Think of Hansel and Gretel. In the first part of the story the parents abandon the children in the forest while saying that they will come back. Since that is not evil enough, the children encounter a person who likes to eat children after burning them alive. A lot of these stories show parts of the human experience that we are better off avoiding. I don't think that tricking your daughter so that you can marry her is a good thing. I don't think that tricking children so that you can eat them is a good thing either. I also don't think that these are simply stories. There likely have been people who did these things or similarly evil behaviors. Do these people fit the stereotypical idea of the ancient person who is connected to Nature and lives a beautiful life? No. These people who are practicing evil are not living a beautiful life. They are not soaking in the gift of beauty and life force that is ever present in the vibrant natural world. They are distracted. They're getting wrapped up in lust or perhaps desperation. They are not accomplishing that goal that I am talking about of being attuned to the world. I bet there were even people who rushed around in an attempt to make their lives better. Distraction, evil, and other barriers to a well-connected and beautiful life were invented long ago. There were also great sadness and loss that people experienced throughout history. I am not the first person who felt numb from grief. That all being said, we do live in unique times. Long ago, it was easier to connect with nature and to live a slower pace of life. In our present moment, it is very difficult. This may sound like a statement that contradicts what I was saying earlier. The point I'm trying to make is that we need to stop making excuses. If it is harder to live attuned to Beauty, then we simply need to do it anyway. Maybe there are ways in which we can experience Beauty even more fully than people did long ago. That sentence may be considered blasphemy by people who idealize the ancient times. The reason I am curious about this is that I think our minds, souls and bodies have greatly evolved overtime. Maybe there are ways in which we experience Beauty in different ways or even better ways than people did long ago. Life was not idyllic in ancient times. There was struggle then and there is struggle now. We need to struggle for what is important, but not push ourselves too hard. This is a very difficult lesson for me to learn. Here I am turning from talking about beauty to talking about fighting for what is good in life. They are similar topics, but a bit different.

We have this idea that if something is easy to attain, then it is not worth very much. This is not true. Some good things will come to us, or we will experience them in some way, and it is a smooth, peaceful, and enjoyable experience to gain these things. Other things we have to fight for. Sometimes we have to fight very hard. The worth of the good thing is not dependent on how easy or hard it is to attain. I used to think that extreme effort led to the greatest Improvement of the world. Now I don't think so. This is a really crucial aspect. We can work ourselves into the ground, literally we can work ourselves to death trying to help the world. Martyrs are still often idealized. Someone who dies from exhaustion and burnout could be considered a martyr even if it is subconsciously. People may not outright say that person is a martyr, but they may feel the same awe and affection towards that person that they would towards a martyr. This is very sick. We lose some of the most beneficial people to this. Whatever your assessment of Rudolf Steiner is, he got burnt out. As he began to get burnt out about 1923, he accelerated his attempts to help the world. He did a tremendous amount of work in 1924 and died in 1925 after finishing about 7k lectures. He was 64. I wish he would have slowed down and tried to live longer. I wish you will slow down. I hope I will slow down too. I still live with some jealousy towards people who work too hard. This is tremendously detrimental. I need to root this out of my being. It is an easy trap to fall into.

In some ways, these tasks like slowing down and connecting with the natural world and beauty are very difficult tasks. I might think that I need to work hard and push myself to achieve these tasks. 10 monasteries are not enough. I need to start by doubling or tripling that number. This is not correct though. You can't push your way into slowing down and relaxing. That is a soft lesson to learn. Soft because we need to be gentle with ourselves. Soft because it involves loving on ourselves so intensely that we melt. Soft because it is more about letting go and just chilling than it is about working hard towards a goal. But chilling and doing nothing productive is blasphemy and unpatriotic; unless you are doing intense meditation for many hours with a very straight spine and your eyes half-open partially focused on a point of the ground about 6 feet in front of where you're sitting. Then you're okay. Just kidding. You're not okay when you aren't allowed to just chill. When you don't allow yourself to chill. So much of what we are able to do or not do in this life depends on what we allow ourselves to do. There are definitely things we should not allow ourselves to do. Righteousness is a good word. It does not belong to any religion or stream of thought. The concept of righteousness is so good that it is righteous. All it means is really good and doing good and not doing harm. That sounds pretty good to me.

The second we realize we are doing harm to ourselves, others, or other things and beings, we need to start on the journey of stopping that activity as quickly as we are able to. Even if we did the activity for years and didn't realize that it was harmful, it is a moral imperative to try to stop doing that activity right away when we do realize that it is harmful. We might be tempted to think that since I did all that harm for all those years, it doesn't really matter if I do this activity for one more day. Actually, it does matter. Knowing and willingly doing harm is astronomically different than not knowing and doing harm out of ignorance. One second of this kind of harm has a huge impact on our own psyche and on anyone else's psyche that finds out we did the harm on purpose. Not only that, but depending on what kind of harm it is, it might have a disastrous effect on that one particular day, if it is something like drunk driving. Even if I think it is not like drunk driving and will only do a tiny little bit of harm, it is actually huge. There is a very sharp line between doing harm without knowing it and doing it on purpose.

Now I want to talk about ice ages. I think that it is a really good idea to continue having them. Once we realize that we already control our climate, we can steer the climate with consciousness instead of steering in a way that is hazardous. First, I want to talk about why we should continue having ice ages, and then I want to touch on how we can manifest the next ice age and all subsequent ice ages. There are two reasons at least that I think we should continue having ice ages. The first involves spirituality and the second involves science. Spiritually speaking, I think it is important for us to continue the cycles of life and experience. The seasons, day and night, and the cycles of the Moon are important for us in a way that goes beyond practical reasons. Spiritually these Cycles are important for us. It is a feeling that I have that they are important. I categorize the Ice Age cycle very similarly to the seasons. There is the Ice Age, the warming age, the heat age, and the cooling age. These correlate to Winter, spring, summer and fall. If we aren't sure how often to have an ice age, I would suggest every 100-200 thousand years. I think this is more or less the background rate. We could start with a low temperature point that more or less matches the average low temperature point of our recent ice ages. Basically, we would create an ice age that pretty much looks like your average Ice Age in the recent past. If we go with the 200k year cycle then 50k years for the Ice Age, 50k years for the warming age, and so on. After a while people could start thinking about whether or not there is an advantage to creating variability in our ice ages and other ages. This could be variability at least in terms of how long the age should last and how high or low to make the temperatures. Let's get to the second reason. Practically speaking, we have no idea what the implications are of stopping a major natural cycle like the ice ages. I like to estimate that Humanity has been through 35 ice ages in 7 million years. Again, if we just stop this natural cycle, we do not know if there will be any adverse effects. Here the precautionary principle comes into play. There could be major disastrous effects of stopping the Ice Age cycle. Perhaps ice ages help to control disease or play some other important role on a practical level. We really don't know and should not be messing with a natural cycle like this. I can't think of any natural cycles that we should be messing with. It seems that we are often doing things with the natural world when we have no idea what the implications will be. Sometimes we introduce a plant or an animal to a new place and it takes over that new place. To me, something like the Ice Ages that affects the whole world is a bigger deal than invasive plants or animals. We shouldn't haphazardly mess with nature, especially on a global scale with ice ages. Feel free to read my book *Philoearth One* to understand how to cool the planet and create an ice age. In that book, I talk about how to move carbon from the atmosphere into the soil by irrigating large areas of land using sprinklers. We would get the water by desalinating ocean water using solar and other renewable energy sources like wave, tide, and wind power. Once you start watering the land, including wilderness areas, you stimulate plant growth. These plants eventually decompose and build up the carbon stored in the soil. I don't know if there are other factors to creating an ice age. I do think that atmospheric carbon levels are a big factor. In order to create an ice age, we would use this technique to pull carbon out of the atmosphere. We would pull a lot of carbon out of the atmosphere and this would probably create an ice age. I'm pretty sure there is nothing else we need to do unless we do something stupid like the volcano simulation to cool the planet. If you are not familiar with this idea it is basically to put some kind of substance in the atmosphere to mimic the explosion of a large volcano. When a large volcano erupts, it temporarily reduces air temperatures. It is a really bad idea, because we are messing with things where we have no understanding of what the impacts will be. So, if we do something stupid like this, then we may need to take additional steps to make an ice age. I have no idea. I just know that we can damage the planet and atmosphere in many ways. We keep inventing new ways to damage the world and ourselves. So, if we do something besides burning fossil fuels and wood that is stupid, we may have additional things to remedy before we can have an ice age.

I believe in continuing the tradition of making fires. On average it would be good if people had one to 3 fires per year. That way we could have fun with the fires, keep traditions like the hand drill and the bow drill alive, and bring people together with the fires like we have been doing for about 0.5-1 million years. That is my rough estimate of how long we have been enjoying the use of fire. Except for these fires, we need to stop burning wood. We also need to stop using wood for buildings and for paper. Old growth forests are really important and also way cool.

So, I want to take a look at some of my old writings. They are mainly from journal entries while I was travelling. Here they are. Like this one.

"Patience is hard. It is developed love and active resistance to anger." 2014
I love that one. Right now, is 2020 so that was about 6 years ago. I was about 30 years old then. I feel

really proud to have written that. Here are some more. I hope you enjoy them.

"I want to create a world where creating beauty is the main occupation of humans."
2008

I'm not going to put quotation marks around all of them, but you can see that I wrote these in the past. Here are more.

I am grateful to myself for working so hard and for learning to let myself relax and not take on more than I am ready for.
2009

I forgive my co-workers for using alcohol/ drugs to socialize and not including me. They were having a good time in the best way they knew and did not know how to include me. I forgive myself for

Philoearth Two

being too shy to instigate community around things that I wanted, although I did do this with music, hot cocoa, food, and aero sports.
2009

I feel strongly that I should be able to ask a driver to slow down or drive safer. It is a basic human right. This is a situation I will probably face in the future. I deserve to be driven safely. I can request something concrete in the most compassionate way, and then be ready for their insecurity to come out and [have myself] not get hot-headed about it. I can always get out as a last resort, but I need to practice dialogue and humility in order to avoid ultimatums.
2009

Why do I care? I care because it feels right to care. It feels dead/

broken/ evil to not care. I do not fully understand it and I do not need to. I don't need a reason to care. I know it is right to care and I do not have to know why.
2008

I want to love without hesitation all beings.
2008

I want to help people.
I will not scoff at this or belittle it or think that it is inevitable. I want to help people.
I want to help people.
I want to help people.
There. So be it. It is so.
2008

I want to write about what spirituality means to me. The quiet feeling that I sometimes get while backpacking. I also feel it sometimes when I am praying or meditating or singing. I feel it at

church. So, it is a feeling and a path. The path part is how I live. Doing things that create the feeling. The feeling feels very right, like pure love. I feel meaningful and that everything around me is meaningful. I feel inspired and like a conduit for love and good energy. My mind slows down when I am feeling spiritual and I feel okay, not stressed or rushed, or wronged or unsatisfied. I feel content with my place in the world.
2008

Wow. That feels really good to share these writings with you. I hope there is something or some things that are useful for you. I love reading, because you get a window into how the author operates, thinks and sees the world. It is so personal. I love writing too. Right now, I am writing my second book. This is my second book you are reading right now. As of right now There is only one person who has read the entirety of my first book Philoearth One besides me. Even though it is only one person, I feel so seen, appreciated and understood. It is so cool that we get to express and also receive expressions from other people. There are so many ways to express, and I hope that more people share with each other through the medium of writing. I think we should do more open mics that are centered on people reading their own writing of all types.

We can also receive expressions from animals and plants. What about rocks? Are they sentient? Can we receive expressions from rocks? Well, I am determined to find out as much as I possibly can about rock sentience. No, really.

My first rock was a generally regular pebble I picked up out of a creek in Switzerland. I had it for a while. I wanted to connect with that rock, so I made a pouch for it out of leather. I had a leather jacket that I got from a thrift store, because I don't want to buy from the new leather industry. It was old and falling apart by the time I got to Switzerland. I cut it up and sewed a little pouch out of the leather for my rock. I also made a leather strap for the pouch so I could put it around my neck so as to connect with the rock and also not lose it. I wasn't particularly thinking about rock sentience then, but more about how much I could notice about the rock over time. Now I am thinking about rock sentience and perhaps I was thinking about it then subconsciously. So right now, I am typing mainly with my right hand for this sentence because I am holding my second rock in my left hand. Ok I put it down. I had the first one for many years. It was 9 sided and kind of a flat pebble so if you held it up like a coin you would see a two dimensional seven-sided shape. It was a great rock. I might still have it in storage. I am not sure. My second rock is a bit smaller and more rounded. I got it about 6 months ago from a beach in California, USA. I really like it. It has a lovely grey color that seems slightly blue. I like to hold it in my hand and also interact with it mainly through the sense of touch. In case you are curious I don't try to taste my rock, but I can do other things like tap it to see what it sounds like. If you want to enjoy having a rock like me, I recommend a regular rock that you would normally think is nothing special. Then hang out with it for a long time and see what you learn or gain. Perhaps if the rock is sentient then you can also give something to the rock, so it is mutually beneficial. This same activity can be done with an animal, a plant, water, the sky, and other objects or non-objects.

So, I want to talk about something. We are in a dire situation. I mean, I think a lot of people know that theoretically, but maybe some people don't let it sink into the visceral feeling realm. I am really worried about the future of Humanity. Basically, I think there is a very real and legitimate possibility that Humanity will go extinct in the next 1 to 2 thousand years. Perhaps sooner, but we have our survival instinct still, so we would find many ways to prolong the lifespan of humanity. Here's the problem with going extinct. It would be no fun. Haha.

We could have way more fun in my opinion if we continued to exist long into the future. We could keep evolving, keep loving others and ourselves, keep discovering things and keep being creative. I feel like if there is some rhyme or reason in the universe, then we are not done with this phase of the party. I do not think this is Earth School so that we learn by suffering and whatnot. I mean we have more life to live as a species. We would be cutting it short.

Here's the other thing, Humanity as it exists now will go extinct someday. Could be millions of years, but not billions. Our Sun will die someday unless it transforms into a different realm. But going by what space researchers say, the Sun has been around about 5 billion years and has another 5 billion to go. I guess they look at other stars and somehow figure out the age of the Sun. I think some of it has to do with the color of the Sun. I'm going to spew some information. It may be correct, or it may be incorrect. I'm not going to look it up right now. If you really want to know about it then go research it yourself. So, when a star is young it is red. As it gets older it goes through a type of rainbow. This rainbow is a little different than the usual color sequence for a rainbow in the sky. First Red, then Orange, then Yellow, then it skips green and instead has White. Then light blue, then dark blue, and then I'm not sure. I think there is a kind of Blue, or White. But you get the idea, you start with Red and then it is similar to a rainbow. Do you know the sky rainbow sequence? Red, Orange, Yellow, Green, Blue, Indigo, and Violet. 7 colors for the sky. On a color wheel it is different. If you don't know what a color wheel is find out for sure. They are so much fun. So, for the color wheel it goes Red, Orange, Yellow, Green, Blue, Purple. 6 colors for the earth. 7 for the sky. Seven is a cosmic, and magical number. 6 is like that but a bit more grounded. Think of the beehive comb. It has little six sided shapes. Very holy but still a bit more earthly than the rainbow. So back to the stars. In my book one, I talked about this color mystery. Then I said go figure it out. Well, I guess I am explaining how I see it now. So, it's pretty cool because, green is the color of life, liveliness, vivacity, verdancy, vividness, aliveness, growth, life force, and generative, creative, birthing, sexual, reproductive aspects. Just think of a spring on the plains. Green, Green Green. It is pretty much right in the middle of the color sequences. I think that is important. I am not sure exactly how, but I think it is being held and taken care of by the powerful colors on each side of it. So anyway, Green is the color of Life on Earth. That's why there are no Green stars. Then!... The flowers are the stars on the Earth. They are so beautiful. Red, Orange, Yellow, White, light Blue and dark Blue. Sounds familiar right. Yep. The exact same colors as the stars. No green flowers in general. They mostly skipped that and stuck with the star colors. So, like I was saying the stars get older and go through that color sequence from Red to Blue. Have you seen the colors in stars? I'm not making up the fact that stars have colors. I promise. Use your favorite search engine and then just go out and have a look. Even without telescopes you can see the colors just with your eyes. Ok, so back to doom and destruction. Remember they don't have Green in the sequence, but White is there instead. So, our star? Our Sun, which is our star, is right about Yellow and White. So, it is transitioning from Yellow to White, then it will continue to Light Blue. I'm not sure about all this. I think this is the way it works, but you might want to double check. It would be fun to learn anyway. So, since we are right in the middle of the color spectrum, then we can understand that the Sun is in the middle of its lifespan. I guess this kind of star lives for 10 billion years. So, we have done 5 billion years and have 5 billion years to go. Actually, that is more about the star than about Humanity. Supposedly, according to the fossil record, Humanity has been around for 7 million years. We could have millions of years to go. In about 250 million years, Earth will be quite uninhabitable. I think that estimate is a bit long. It might be sooner, but either way you get the idea, some number of millions of years, but not billions, even though our star may live billions. There are so many things I want to say. I want to talk about how the Sun goes around the galaxy. I want to talk about when we discovered how to use fire. I want to talk about the possibility of changing realms. I also want to get back to the beginning of this section where I was talking about feeling this dire situation. I also want to talk about religions and holidays.

Maybe I should continue by talking about the dire situation. So, we could have millions of years to live, but we might cut it short in the next 2 thousand years. Fuck that. That is no fun. That is bad. I think good is good and bad is bad. In general. There is a lot of disagreement about what is good and bad, but if you think about growing flowers vs raping children, you see what I am getting at. So, we can do better than letting this whole thing go like that. That concept that we are doomed, and it is all pointless is pretty messed up. Do not give up on yourself; and don't give up on Humanity; and don't give up on life, growth, beauty and all good things. Never give up. It's not allowed. Haha. But really. Be righteous. Love the good. Don't give up. There is a magic in the firm stance that you will not give up. I will not give up and that is unshakable. There is magic in that. People say, over my dead body. That is very accurate. As long as you live you can fight for something. You get to choose what you fight for. Please don't give up on Humanity. Ok I think I made my point.

Ok, so we have the technique for fixing climate change with desalinated water. We have a look at how long Humanity could live and how that is way more fun than cutting the party short. And we have the love of ourselves and Humanity buried in our hearts. Let's let it out.

I want to talk about Religions. They are pretty cool, except when they get out of control. We have these concepts of what the different religions are, but really you can identify as whatever and make up what that means to you. So, you can make your own conception of a specific religion or multiple religions or the absence of religion. People will have their preconceived ideas and baggage about what the concept means to them. Then there can be communication and idea sharing. For example, I have spent many years involved in the United Church of Christ. I have also been several times to a Baptist Church. The idea of what Christianity is in those two places is very different from each other. There are many beautiful things in both places, but one difference is that the UCC allows people to join even if they identify with a different religion. At least this is my experience in multiple UCC churches. I think technically you could join a Baptist church and identify with a different religion, but I'm pretty sure it would be considered odd and not encouraged. Anyway, there are many interpretations of what Christianity is. Some focus on the cross and the resurrection. Other's focus on the life and teachings of

Jesus. Some actively support gay/queer people, some actively discourage people from being gay/queer. Some probably say it is none of their business and religion is not about that kind of thing. We need to support gay/queer people completely and without any question or hesitation. To be affirming not just accepting. This is a great example of religion getting out of control. The theories and teachings become practical and social, and then all of a sudden, gay/queer people are getting beat up or whatever. Hate done in the name or religion. That is fucked up. Another example is when nationalism/tribalism gets enmeshed with religion. Our God could beat your God up! You get the idea. Ok so enough about what is bad about religion. What is good about it? So much. So much love and service has been done in association with religion. So much community and relationship building. So much inner work and healing for aching hearts. Ok so a while back I said I didn't think I would ever pick a religion. I am still mostly that way. I read Hindu Vedas for fun and try to read every word in the book of numbers in the bible. Haha. It's pretty great to identify as multireligious or agnostic. You get to do whatever you want. Haha. Well, that is true no matter what you identify with, but it is easier if you are saying you are multireligious or agnostic in my experience. Ok so here we go. I am choosing to identify as Pagan in certain situations. It is kind of exciting and kind of overwhelming. Right away I seem to want to make conditional statements like how I may not follow every tradition that most Pagans follow. Ok. Whatever. I am a multireligious, agnostic

Pagan. There we have it. Pagan for short. Haha. The neat thing is that by identifying with a concept, like Paganism, you open doors in social situations. Someone might feel comfortable talking about certain things like the life force of a tree or connecting with a tree. They might feel more comfortable talking about this to a Pagan than to a Christian or person of another religious identification. There can also be camaraderie. Like oooo. Let's do some Pagan tradition together! Ok so that leads me to Pagan traditions and holidays.

Here is my understanding and how I celebrate holidays. I celebrate 9 holidays. 4 following the cycle of the Sun's light. 4 following the cycle of the Earth's warmth and 1 for the Moon. The first four are somewhat well known. They are the two solstices and the two equinoxes. Then there are the four about the cycle of warmth. This lags behind the cycle of light a bit. You know how August is hot, but the day with the most light is in June. So, the warmth cycle lags behind the light cycle. Ok so the 4 warmth holidays are kind of like the solstice and equinoxes. They are exactly halfway between the light solstices and equinoxes. I think of it as August 1st being approximately the hottest day, so it is like a heat solstice. It is also exactly halfway between the summer light solstice and the fall light equinox. So, you divide the year into 8 equal parts. I will get to the moon holiday later. Some of the warmth holidays are well known. The most popular warmth holiday in the United States is Halloween. It is exactly halfway between fall equinox and winter solstice. Then we have the winter solstice. Then we have a holiday on Feb 2 called Imbolc in I think the Celtic tradition. Then spring equinox. Then May day. Then Summer Solstice. Then a holiday on August 1st called Lughnasadh. Then fall equinox and then back to Halloween. Those are the 8 holidays that follow the light and warmth cycles. Then we have the moon holiday I celebrate. It has many names, but I call it Ēostre. People usually say it is the 1st full moon after the spring equinox, but I like to say it is the 4th full moon of the year. Let me explain. I see the year as mainly beginning on the winter solstice which I consider to be the longest night of the year. Actually, it is a moment where imaginary lines continuing out from the earth's axis and the Sun's axis touch. Imagine you have a line through the earth from pole to pole. This is the earth's axis. The Sun has the same thing. Then make those lines longer in both directions. The imaginary lines only cross at the moments of the summer and winter solstices. So once that moment occurs, which is the same as the moment the modern space scientists say is the solstice, then we start counting the full moons. 4th full moon is Ēostre. This is almost always the same as the 1st full moon after the spring equinox, but not always. The reason I like the 4th full moon idea is that I think it may be how it was originally done. That is just my theory. That people from many different lands would communicate and spread the news of when the 1st full moon of the year was. Then by the time the 4th full moon came around everyone would have heard what moon we were on so everyone could celebrate Ēostre. So, let's get into some traditions. For Halloween, the dressing up, the jack o'lanterns and the treats are all pre-Christian. So, let's go through the year. Then comes winter solstice and you can make wands. Then comes Imbolc. You wake up early and dig a little hole in the cold ground. You put a wick in it and pour your candle directly into the ground. Then you light it! Then comes Spring equinox.

Before we continue with the traditions, I wanted to say something that is on my mind today. I am just starting to write for the day, and this is what I am thinking about. Don't belittle your gifts. I was thinking about this in relation to my writing. My writing is one of my gifts. I think it is less about being the best writer or even being a high-quality writer. I think it is more about giving your gifts. The things you want to share and give to the world. I am putting a lot of time and energy into my writing. I am giving a gift to the world and I am proud of that. You remember how many people have read my first book as of today besides me? One person. If I let that outward circumstance direct my gift giving, I would have given up long ago. Don't give up. Give your gifts. You know how much better the world would be if people were proud of their gifts and did not belittle them? Way better. People shy away from giving their gifts for many reasons, but I think a big one is feeling insecure about their gifts. Are my gifts good enough? That is so terrible. That is the wrong way to think. The good way to think is that your gifts are good. They are gifts after all. So just give them and try very hard. The world will be so much better. Think of all the other people in the world and if they fully gave their gifts. You would be glad that they were doing that. So, feel the same way about yourself.

Ok, back to holidays. So, we were on Spring equinox. For that one I like to make a plate of treats for the nature spirits. All of these traditions I got from somewhere. I don't remember where, but I didn't make them up. So, you can put whatever you want on the plate. Maybe a little bit of something sweet. I like to put many things, but just tiny bits of each thing. Things that you like. I put a little corn chip. Also a few raisins. Put some little herbs or spices. Maybe a flower. So, you make this plate of goodies and then you take it out into nature and leave it for the nature spirits. If you are leaving it in the forest somewhere then don't leave your plate. Maybe set each item on the ground or on a log or something. I love this tradition. Ok next. Eggs,

eggs, eggs. Haha. If you are vegan, then you can skip the eggs part or carve wooden eggs. The other thing for Ēostre is to eat some bitter herbs and make a wish. As I said, I like to celebrate Ēostre on the 4th full moon after the winter solstice. This is usually a bit after Spring equinox. So, you can paint eggs, do an egg hunt where you hide eggs and then look for them, or you can paint wooden eggs. Just don't waste too many eggs. Maybe just paint one egg or if you are dying them use natural food coloring and do a quick egg hunt so they are still good to eat. For the herbs, you can cook some bitter herbs for a meal like mustard greens. Then when you are ready to make your wish, eat a little bit of the greens or a bit of oregano or any bitter herb and make a wish. I wouldn't tell people what your wish is, but if someone says their wish, it is not the end of the world. Ok, on to May Day. For this one you make a maypole. Just do some research. You will need long, thick, strong ribbons and a big pole. I usually bury the base of the pole in the ground and then dig it up after May day. Then there are many complicated dances to do with the may pole. You can have different numbers of ribbons, but I sometimes do 6. A good way to get started is to have all 6 or whatever number people circle the may pole holding their ribbons. Just have everyone go the same direction until the ribbons run out and then unwind. Make music too. Ok, then summer solstice. Drum and dance. I would refrain from making a fire for several reasons. One is that there is more wildfire danger in the summer. Another reason is that I think it is good to make a fire or two in the winter when it is cold. Making too many fires will make climate change worse. I don't think it needs to be on a particular holiday. Just make a fire or two in the winter and have fun. I once made a big fire out in the forest with some friends during a snowstorm out in the wilderness. Snow was all on the ground and it was snowing significantly. We had to all hover over the flame at first like a big sphere protecting it. Then we made the fire 9 feet high. Ok so no need to make a fire on summer solstice. People used to do that but that was before climate change. Besides, you don't really need the warmth in the summer. So then comes Lughnasadh. For that one you can make berry bracelets and give them to people. Just find a way. Maybe using cooking twine if you want to be careful about what kind of string you are using. Then the person who gets the berry bracelet puts it on and then eats it while wearing it. Ok, on to fall equinox. For this one I like to make grain art. Then we are back to Halloween! So, there are the 9 holidays that I celebrate mainly. There are also good social holidays, like indigenous peoples day and carfree day.

So, let's talk about the possibility of changing realms. Here is what I really want to say about that. I don't know for sure if we can change realms or not change realms before, during or after the extinction of Humanity as we know it. I am sure that humanity as we know it will go extinct within the next quarter billion years like I was saying earlier due to the Sun changing. That has been a hard thing for me to come to terms with. I really think we should not cut the party short just because the party will end someday. Ok, but does the party really end? That is the present question, and I am saying emphatically that I don't have the answer. I am honestly pretty sure that no one does. This gets into the question of afterlife and reincarnation. Just as a single human being may have an afterlife or a reincarnation, so humanity may have an afterlife or a reincarnation. I hope you are paying attention because this is important. Many people think that since many of us believe that we cannot know if there is an afterlife, then what is the point of trying to make life better if it is all going to end someday anyway. Ok this is crucial. It doesn't matter if it will end or not. It doesn't matter if it will end or not end in terms of whether or not to care about life and all things living. There. That is my point. I am confident that spirituality exists, but even if I am wrong and it does not exist, then think of the person you love the most or the kind of plant or animal you love the most. Then think of them getting killed or hurt in some way. Does that make you sad? Of course it does. So, life matters to you. That is all you need to know. You don't need to know if life has inherent worth, which I am telling you it does. You simply need to know that life matters to you. Now if life does not matter to you and there is nothing that you love, then you are ill, but you can heal.

I mentioned before that I want to talk about how the Sun goes around the center of the galaxy. I find it fascinating. It turns out the Sun has gone around about 20 times since it was born. Some people call the time it takes to go around once a galactic year. I prefer to use a word that is not in much use yet, which is "helia". The Sun is 20 helias old and has about another 20 helias to go.

I also said that I wanted to talk about the discovery of using fire. There are different estimates of when this happened. I think that a good estimate is 0.5-1 million years ago. It may have been earlier or later, but this gives us an idea of when this happened. As a few points of reference, one estimate for humanity evolving from an ancestral primate is 7 million years ago. One estimate for the invention of boats to use for travelling is 40 thousand years ago. One estimate for the advent of painting on cave walls is 25 thousand years ago. This slowly developed into writing, which is estimated to have come to fruition 5 thousand years ago. What I am getting at is that the use of fire goes way way back. Half a million years back probably or more. That is way older than boats or cave paintings, at least semi-permanent cave paintings. I think the estimate about the boats has to do with when people arrived at Australia and other places you could not swim to.

So, we have this old tradition of making fires. Before, I talked about an ice age coming every 100-200k years. If we estimate that an ice age comes once every 100k years, then we have used fire during the last 5 or more ice ages. This may not be exact, but you get a rough idea of how many ice ages we had before and after beginning to use fire. Our last ice age was a pretty cold one and got down to about 6 degrees Celsius, compared with the prior ice age which got down to about 7 degrees Celsius. Both cold

I know. This temperature I am saying was the global average temperature for many years during each respective ice age. As a point of reference, the heat age between those two ice ages got up to about 13 degrees Celsius. So 150k years ago we were in an ice age. Then about 100k years ago we were in a heat age. Then 20k years ago we were in our most recent ice age. Remember that the ice ages don't operate like clockwork. Some are a bit longer and some a bit shorter. So 20k years ago we were at 6 degrees Celsius. Then 10k years ago we were already in a heat age which is our present age. The temperature 10k years ago was 13 degrees Celsius just like the top of the last heat age. So, we have ice age 7 degrees Celsius, heat age 13 degrees Celsius, ice age 6 degrees Celsius, and then our present heat age at 13 degrees

Celsius. That was 10k years ago that we were already at 13 degrees Celsius. So up until recently we have not seen a major warming trend due to the advent of fire use. Just a slow overall decline in temperature from 24 degrees Celsius when dinosaurs went extinct to about 9 or 10 degrees Celsius as a midline between our recent ice ages and heat ages. Let's call it 10 degrees Celsius. 10 is normal now. 7 is an ice age. 13 is a heat age.

Ok so we used fire from about 0.5 million years ago to 10 thousand years ago without any noticeable effects on the global average temperature. The temperature declined since dinosaurs went extinct instead of rising. The carbon from the fires that was released to the atmosphere did not cause a noticeable warming effect.

Since 10k years ago the picture is a bit different.

Let's jump ahead to the last 100 years. These days the burning of carbon continues but on a larger scale. Long ago it was pretty much just wood and maybe other plant matter like grass or leaves that we burned. These days it is wood, coal and oil mainly. The concept is actually very similar. We were burning carbon then and we are burning carbon now. Just we are burning a lot more wood, and have also added coal and oil to the picture. Deforestation, erosion and livestock also contribute to the carbon in the atmosphere, but let's focus on the burning right now.

So here is what happened recently. Remember 10k years ago we were at 13 degrees Celsius in our current heat age. 13 degrees

Celsius is supposed to be just about the peak and the turnaround point to then go back down to an ice age of about 7 degrees Celsius. Instead, the temperature rose one degree Celsius over the next 5k years from 13 to 14. So 10k years ago 13 degrees Celsius and 5k years ago 14 degrees Celsius. Then we wavered a bit but pretty much just stayed at about 14 degrees Celsius.

Now it is really important to understand the last 100 years and how that compares to the last 60 million years. It is good to actually look at the global average temperature graphs for the last 100 years. You will see that the gradual change in temperature changes into a rapidly rising temperature. Here's the take home. In the last 75 years we have had our global average temperature go up by one degree Celsius.

Boom. That is a big deal. That is like the holy grail of climate science. You heard it here first folks. Well, maybe not, but it is still important. Remember that it took 5k years to go from 13 degrees Celsius to 14 degrees Celsius. Then we raised the temperature from 14 degrees Celsius to 15 degrees Celsius in the last 75 years.

I would go so far as to say that a one degree rise per 75 years is the new normal for now. As a reference, when humanity evolved 7 million years ago the temperature was 17 degrees Celsius. That was part way between 24 degrees Celsius when dinosaurs went extinct and 10 degrees Celsius in more recent times.

If we keep up this pace, we will be back at 17 degrees Celsius in 150 years. Honestly, that would be terrible, but it would not make us go extinct. We could survive as a species at 17 degrees Celsius. What is concerning to me is two things. One is that we keep up this pace and fry the whole planet and ourselves in the next 1-2k years. In 1k years we would rise 13 degrees to 28 degrees Celsius and in 2k years we would be toasty toast.

The other possibility that really concerns me is if we just raise the temperature significantly and then don't ever cool it down. As I mentioned before, we might have widespread disease and suffering due to a significantly hotter planet. So, I highly recommend that we start cooling the planet as soon as ethically possible. The wealthy countries should reduce carbon burning more than the poor countries. So, we have this ability now to control the climate and I hope we will learn to use it wisely.

Normally we would burn plants/carbon when we want to create a heat age and we would water plants when we want to create an ice age. A good starting place would be to go up to 13 degrees Celsius for our heat ages and go down to 8 degrees Celsius for our ice ages. Let's get to that watering!

One important thing about the watering is that it should be done in such a way that it encourages the migration of native plants. If you take the Sahara Desert as an example, there is the southern border of the desert which pretty much stretches across all of the African continent. So, at that border you have the desert and then just south of that you have the savanna. South of the savanna you have forest and south of the forest you have rainforest. So, we would water swaths of land with sprinklers. As a side note I think it is good to have the sprinklers set to spray downhill with about a 135-degree angle to prevent erosion. You don't want to water too much to where you are rapidly and drastically changing the plant species of the ecosystem. You want to slowly move the native plants north. Slowly each ecosystem moves north in this example. The desert becomes savanna, the savanna becomes forest, and the forest becomes rainforest. Slowly you give new life to the desert region. We also need to talk about rural and urban landscapes. Also, there is the topic of desert preservation.

Let's talk about desert preservation first. In order to significantly reduce the carbon in the atmosphere we need to do a significant amount of watering. Right now the deserts are spreading. This is called desertification. The world is drying up. We need to reverse this process and shrink the deserts. That being said, deserts are great ecosystems, and we need to take desert preservation into account. It would be terrible if the whole Sahara Desert disappeared. So, the idea is that we shrink the desert until it is a reasonable size and then set up conservation measures to preserve that desert. It is important to take into account the plants and wildlife, as well as the cultural areas of the deserts. That being said, we should really shrink the Sahara Desert until it is 10 to 20 percent of its current size. I think it is a similar picture for the huge desert area in the center of Australia. For smaller deserts we might want to keep a larger percentage.

Ok, let's talk about urban and rural landscapes. It is a similar situation to the wilderness areas. We want to stimulate plant growth. In fact, it may be wise to start with the urban and rural areas, because some people will be resistant to the idea of installing sprinklers in wilderness areas. Even so, we should definitely do wilderness irrigation within the next 50 years, probably a lot sooner. That being said, starting with urban and rural areas is still a good idea. Currently we have 16k desalination facilities in the world. We need to make a lot of improvements with the desalination so that it is more ecological. As we do that, we can greatly increase the worldwide capacity for desalination without significantly harming the environment.

Greatly increasing the freshwater supply on a global scale will be great for human, animal and plant uses. Don't forget about mushrooms and other lifeforms. If we start with urban centers, then using native plants is great, but not quite as essential as out in the wilderness. We can plant ornamentals such as roses, and food crops such as fruit trees. We can also use some of the water for human use like drinking and bathing. We still need to conserve water and use grey water systems so that a good portion of the water gets to the plants.

Rural landscapes are like a mixture of the urban areas and wilderness. It is more important to have native plants in rural areas than in the urban centers. This is important for pollinators and wildlife. Human habitat is a huge part of the planet. We need to shrink the human habitat. I want to talk more about the human habitat, but for now let's focus on the rural landscapes.

A lot of rural areas are focused on agriculture. The key here is to use more water in the farming practices, without contributing to the problem of super weeds. That doesn't mean wasting water to evaporation. The pros and cons of drip tape should be taken into consideration. Drip tape does not lose very much water to evaporation. Let's talk about superweeds first and then talk about shrinking the human habitat.

We are currently making superweeds by the way we farm.

This is hard to get around. Anytime you pull up a weed, or spray it, or cut it at the base, or whatever you do to it, it gets smarter. The weeds develop ways to propagate with less root left or with a more toxic spray applied or whatever. They evolve. We are literally cultivating super weeds even in organic farms. The concern here is that we may run out of ways to get the weeds to go away, because they will get so strong and smart. It may be hundreds of years, but it could ruin agriculture in general, causing mass starvation. So, what to do?

The answer is that you have to pretty much stop fighting the weeds and take a whole new approach. This approach may take 2 to 20 times as much land space for a given yield. Basically, you would rely more on native plant food sources, kind of like a cross between agriculture and native plant restoration. Lots of oak trees. You need lots of oak trees. My local tribe of Native Americans have a history of eating acorns for more than 75 percent of their food source. Acorns are just a staple like potatoes or wheat. You could make acorn pasta or pizza or whatever you need to feel awesome. Ok, then there are manzanita berries. There are 95 species of manzanita native to California. Let's make some manzanita sweets. Don't forget about pine nuts! You get the idea. Lots more land, lots more time, and lots more effort towards sustainability rather than convenience. Mushrooms, berries, apple trees, oooo I love black raspberries, and we can grow some kinds of tubers. I don't know which types would be best or if we have some native tubers. I am talking about California, USA, but the concept can be applied everywhere. Ok no more super weeds.

Ok we need to shrink the human habitat. In order to do that we should shrink the human population to about 1 billion people by people voluntarily choosing to have fewer children. We can also live more densely. I think one of the things that makes people want to spread out and not live densely is sex. People love sex, but are so embarrassed about other people hearing them have sex. So, we either get over ourselves and listen to loud sex, or we need to build soundproof rooms in housing structures. Don't believe it could work? I know someone who shot a gun into a big bean bag in one room that was super soundproofed, and their friend could not hear it hardly at all in the next room. Really. I think we need to overcome this obstacle if we are going to save the planet and ourselves. We need to shrink the human habitat, and to do so we need to live densely, and to do that we need to soundproof rooms. Ok. Besides that, we just need to be creative and build up rather than out and whatnot.

Ok. Another thing. We really need ecological desalination. This is very important. Why ruin the planet while trying to save the planet? So, there are at least three aspects. The intake, the salt output, and the toxins. For the intake we need to find ways to not kill so many forms of sea life when we suck the water in. Like perhaps having really big screens instead of small ones. I don't know. We just need to engineer it so that it is not sucking in so hard and so that we don't kill as much sea life.

About the salt output, I understand that we are pumping very salty water back out into the ocean, which then kills lots of sea life. So, we should be able to overcome this, and either dehydrate the salt or make it almost dehydrated and dispose of it somewhere other than the ocean.

About the toxins, we just have to find cleaner ways of doing it. I'm pretty sure evaporative desal is more energy intensive, but that may be the way to go or some other way that is low in toxic waste. So, for sure ecological desal is more expensive and there are already people working on this topic. What we need is a funding program that awards grants of some sort to desal plants that are implementing or transitioning to ecological desal.

Basically, you need a non-profit that certifies the plants worldwide. They could get different levels of certification based on specific criteria. I think it would be good to have a rating system that can easily evolve. Like the first plant that is certified could get a 45-point rating. Then as the criteria evolve, there could be higher and lower levels. So maybe the next plant is a lower level, and it gets 35 points. Then over time there may be even more specific criteria so smaller increments of points would be used. For instance, a plant could attain a level 38. c I love math and think it should help us evolve rather than restrict us.

Maybe a plant that is upgrading to a higher rating could get foundational grants to help with that process. We have 16k desal plants in the world. We need to incentivize them to upgrade to ecological desal and incentivize sustainability of all types for the new ones. Also, we need to take the renewable power into account with the rating system.

Ok here's my pep talk. Go get 'em tiger! Pep talk over. Hope you have a great day. Lot's of love,
Brendan